HS◉
HOMELAND SE
OPERATIONAL ANALYSI

Practical Terrorism Prevention

Executive Summary

BRIAN A. JACKSON, ASHLEY L. RHOADES, JORDAN R. REIMER, NATASHA LANDER,
KATHERINE COSTELLO, SINA BEAGHLEY

Published in 2019

Preface

As part of an overall reexamination of terrorism prevention (superseding the programs and activities previously known as countering violent extremism [CVE]) policy, the U.S. Department of Homeland Security (DHS) asked the Homeland Security Operational Analysis Center (HSOAC) to examine the state of knowledge regarding terrorism prevention organization, coordination, programming, and policy. HSOAC was tasked to examine past CVE and current terrorism prevention efforts by DHS and its interagency partners, and explore options for this policy area going forward.

This document summarizes the findings that are fully documented in the companion report, *Practical Terrorism Prevention: Reexamining U.S. National Approaches to Addressing the Threat of Ideologically Motivated Violence.*

These findings should be of interest to policymakers at the federal, state, and local levels; members of organizations with interests in terrorism prevention activities; civil rights and civil liberties organizations; and the broader public.

This research was sponsored by the Office of Policy, DHS, and conducted within the Strategy, Policy, and Operations Program of the HSOAC federally funded research and development center (FFRDC).

Comments or questions about this report should be addressed to the project leaders, Brian A. Jackson and Sina Beaghley, at bjackson@rand.org and beaghley@rand.org, respectively.

About the Homeland Security Operational Analysis Center

The Homeland Security Act of 2002 (Section 305 of Public Law 107-296, as codified at 6 U.S.C. § 185), authorizes the Secretary of Homeland Security, acting through the Under Secretary for Science and Technology, to establish one or more FFRDCs to provide independent analysis of homeland security issues. The RAND Corporation operates HSOAC as an FFRDC for DHS under contract HSHQDC-16-D-00007.

The HSOAC FFRDC provides the government with independent and objective analyses and advice in core areas important to the Department in support of policy development, decisionmaking, alternative approaches, and new ideas on issues of significance. The HSOAC FFRDC also works with and supports other federal, state, local, tribal, and public- and private-sector organizations that make up the homeland security enterprise. The HSOAC FFRDC's research is undertaken by mutual consent with DHS and is organized as a set of discrete tasks. This report presents the results of research and analysis conducted under Task Order HSHQDC-17-J-00532, titled "Terrorism Prevention Study and Threat Prevention and Security Policy Support."

The results presented in this report do not necessarily reflect official DHS opinion or policy.

For more information on HSOAC, see www.rand.org/hsoac.

For more information on this publication, visit www.rand.org/t/RR2647z2.

Contents

Figures and Tables

Figures

Tables

Abbreviations

9/11	September 11, 2001, terrorist attacks
CAB	Community Awareness Briefing
CREX	Community Resilience Exercise
CVE	Countering Violent Extremism
DHS	Department of Homeland Security
DOJ	Department of Justice
DOS	Department of State
FBI	Federal Bureau of Investigation
FY	fiscal year
HSOAC	Homeland Security Operational Analysis Center
ISIS	Islamic State of Iraq and Syria
NCTC	National Counterterrorism Center
NGO	nongovernmental organization
P2P	Peer2Peer
PIRUS	Profiles of Individual Radicalization in the United States
RAN	Radicalisation Awareness Network
START	National Consortium for the Study of Terrorism and Responses to Terrorism

Executive Summary

Terrorism prevention policy and programs aim to reduce the risk of terrorism by applying tools and approaches *other than* the traditional law enforcement and criminal justice tools of arrest, prosecution, and incarceration. Current federal terrorism prevention efforts subsume past activities referred to as countering violent extremism (CVE), including such efforts as countering extremist messages online, community engagement by law enforcement and other organizations, and educating community members to recognize warning signs of radicalization to violence. Consistent with the *National Strategy for Counterterrorism*, current terrorism prevention efforts emphasize building effective partnerships between law enforcement, civil society, social service agencies, and communities. In the United States, the development of policy in this area has focused on the local radicalization to violence of individuals exposed to extremist content on the internet, citizens interacting with representatives of terrorist organizations abroad, and attacks and attempted attacks by individuals inspired either by foreign terrorist organizations or by ideologies of domestic origin.

Current terrorism prevention and past CVE efforts in the United States have been controversial. Since these efforts often respond to activities that are not crimes, there are serious concerns regarding the potential to infringe on constitutionally protected rights, stigmatize individuals and communities, or damage trust between the government and the public. It is difficult to know who to focus on for terrorism prevention efforts, given that there are no unambiguous early indicators of future violent behavior and limited means available to distinguish those individuals who *appear to be threats* from those who *actually do pose a threat*. Past CVE efforts have been criticized for focusing disproportionately on Muslim communities—creating both stigma and prejudice. Critics have accused the government of using these programs as veiled surveillance to support enforcement action, in large part by encouraging community members to spy on one another (American Civil Liberties Union, undated), rather than serving as alternatives to enforcement action.

Designing effective terrorism prevention efforts while addressing the concerns they raise is complicated by the fact that many different entities and organizations have roles in this space. CVE in the United States has been an interagency effort, with four federal security-focused agencies—the U.S. Department of Homeland Security (DHS), U.S. Department of Justice (DOJ), Federal Bureau of Investigation (FBI), and National Counterterrorism Center (NCTC)—playing the most-central roles, and with varied levels of involvement from other agencies. Nongovernmental organizations (NGOs) and other entities also have played important roles in past CVE efforts and likely will have to do so in the future for national terrorism prevention efforts to succeed. In fact, engagement and intervention efforts often need the help of local organizations and require access to such capabilities as mental health services, employment assistance, and other capacities maintained by nonprofit and service organizations.

Focus of This Study

The complexity and controversy associated with both past CVE and current terrorism prevention efforts have catalyzed a spirited debate about which programs are appropriate, which agencies should participate, how information should be collected and shared, and the balance between the intended benefits of such programs and their unintended consequences. In support of DHS planning and strategy development efforts, the Office of Policy asked the Homeland Security Operational Analysis Center (HSOAC), a federally funded research and development center operated by the RAND Corporation, to examine the state of knowledge regarding terrorism prevention in the United States and to develop policy options for this area.

This study sought to learn from past CVE efforts and to explore possible paths forward to *effective*, but also *practical*, federal and national terrorism prevention. Our focus in this study was explicitly on *policies and programs within the United States*, responding to terrorism risk inspired by ideologies emerging out of international or foreign-origin terrorist threats to the country and from homegrown sources. Our focus was also explicitly *federal*: Although we looked at available local programming, including nongovernmental efforts, our primary goal was to identify lessons relevant to shaping federal policy. We also focused specifically on terrorism prevention activities related to *violence—not beliefs*—since individuals' freedoms of belief, religion, and political view are protected. We also distinguish *terrorism prevention* from the operational and enforcement actions taken by law enforcement organizations, although law enforcement or criminal justice agencies may be centrally involved in terrorism prevention efforts.

The study drew on multiple sources and approaches, including

- a review of published literature on terrorism prevention and CVE as well as material on current efforts and programs
- interviews with current and former members of federal organizations with expertise in terrorism prevention or CVE
- discussions with other researchers who had studied the topic

- interviews with members of the technology industry and associated nonprofits related to online extremism concerns
- field visits with state, local, and nongovernmental organizations in five U.S. cities[1] supporting case studies of metropolitan areas in different parts of the country
- case studies of seven countries' efforts[2]
- an examination of publicly available open-source threat information.

The project involved approximately 100 discussions with about 175 individuals.

This document summarizes key findings and policy options resulting from our study. It is divided into five parts:

- The Nature of the Homeland Terrorist Threat
- Current Terrorism Prevention Policies and Capabilities
- Resources Allocated to Terrorism Prevention Efforts
- Integration of Terrorism Prevention Efforts
- Federal Options to Strengthen Terrorism Prevention Capability.

The Nature of the Homeland Terrorist Threat

In order to design effective terrorism prevention programs, we must begin with the nature and parameters of the threat those efforts are seeking to address. An understanding of the threat provides a baseline for assessing whether terrorism prevention efforts are adequate and serves as a point of departure for determining what types of additional terrorism prevention programming are needed.

Mass-casualty attacks have been prominent in national experience of terrorism, including the 1995 bombing of the Alfred P. Murrah Federal Building in Oklahoma City that killed 168 people and the September 11, 2001 (9/11), attacks that resulted in the death of almost 3,000 individuals and the injury of many more people, including those with long-term health effects from the attacks themselves and from subsequent response operations. 9/11 galvanized the national response to terrorism, leading to the formation of DHS, among other national actions and policy changes. DHS is charged with addressing not just the risk of similar large-scale attacks, but also smaller-scale, and more-frequent terrorist threats. Although the potential for individuals to radicalize to violence had previously raised concern, efforts in the wake of 9/11 built the foun-

---

[1]   The cities were Boston, Massachusetts; Denver, Colorado; Houston, Texas; Los Angeles, California; and Minneapolis-St. Paul, Minnesota.

[2]   The countries were Australia, Belgium, Canada, Denmark, France, Germany, and the United Kingdom. The case studies were analyzed to identify both lessons from single countries (experiences that were parallel to terrorism prevention challenges encountered by the United States or seemed particularly relevant to U.S. circumstances) and across groups of countries.

dation for CVE in the United States and the subsequent expansion in the succeeding years.

Ideological Sources of Threat

Although large-scale attacks like 9/11 and the threat of attack from al Qaeda and subsequently ISIS[3] have shaped recent national responses to terrorism, the history of terrorism in the United States is a long one. Over decades, the country has experienced attacks originating from groups and individuals inspired by varied ideologies and pursuing vastly different goals through violence. Drawing on data from the National Consortium for the Study of Terrorism and Responses to Terrorism (START) Profiles of Individual Radicalization in the United States (PIRUS) database,[4] Figure 1 shows how the ideological sources of terrorist threats have shifted over time. Although some elements of the threat landscape have remained relatively stable over time (e.g., white supremacism), others have changed significantly from one decade to the next (e.g., the surge in Islamist radicalization from the 1980s to the present).

Geographic Distribution of Recent Incidents of Radicalization

Drawing on the same START PIRUS data discussed above to characterize the ideological sources of radicalization and mobilization to violence, it is also clear that such incidents have not been limited to one part of the country in the years since 9/11. According to the database, between 2002 and 2016, 943 individuals were radicalized in the United States, with 382 (roughly 40 percent) of these cases occurring in 2012 or later (START, undated[b]). The individuals radicalized through a mix of ideologies: 47 percent were Islamist, 37 percent were far-right, 9 percent were single-issue, and 8 percent were far-left.[5] Incidents of radicalization included in PIRUS have been spread across the United States. Figure 2 maps those incidents of radicalization in 2002–2016 by city-state pair of the residence location of the individuals for all ideological motivations. Instances of radicalization have occurred in virtually all 50 states, in both

---

[3]   The organization's name transliterates from Arabic as al-Dawlah al-Islamiyah fi al-'Iraq wa al-Sham (abbreviated as Da'ish or DAESH). In the West, it is commonly referred to as the Islamic State of Iraq and the Levant (ISIL), the Islamic State of Iraq and Syria, the Islamic State of Iraq and the Sham (both abbreviated as ISIS), or simply as the Islamic State (IS). Arguments abound as to which is the most accurate translation, but here we refer to the group as ISIS.

[4]   PIRUS defines its inclusion criteria as ". . . a sample of individuals espousing Islamist, far right, far left, or single-issue ideologies who have radicalized within the United States to the point of committing ideologically motivated illegal violent or non-violent acts, joining a designated terrorist organization, or associating with an extremist organization whose leader(s) has/have been indicted of an ideologically motivated violent offense." See START, 2018. According to the START website, examples of single-issue extremists in the database include "individuals associated with the Puerto Rican independence movement, anti-abortion extremists that were not motivated by traditional far right issues (anti-government, race superiority, etc.), members of the Jewish Defense League, and extremists with idiosyncratic ideologies (e.g., Ted Kaczynski)." See START, undated(b).

[5]   The percentages do not add to 100 percent due to rounding.

Figure 1
Ideological Basis for Radicalization of Individuals in the United States, by Decade

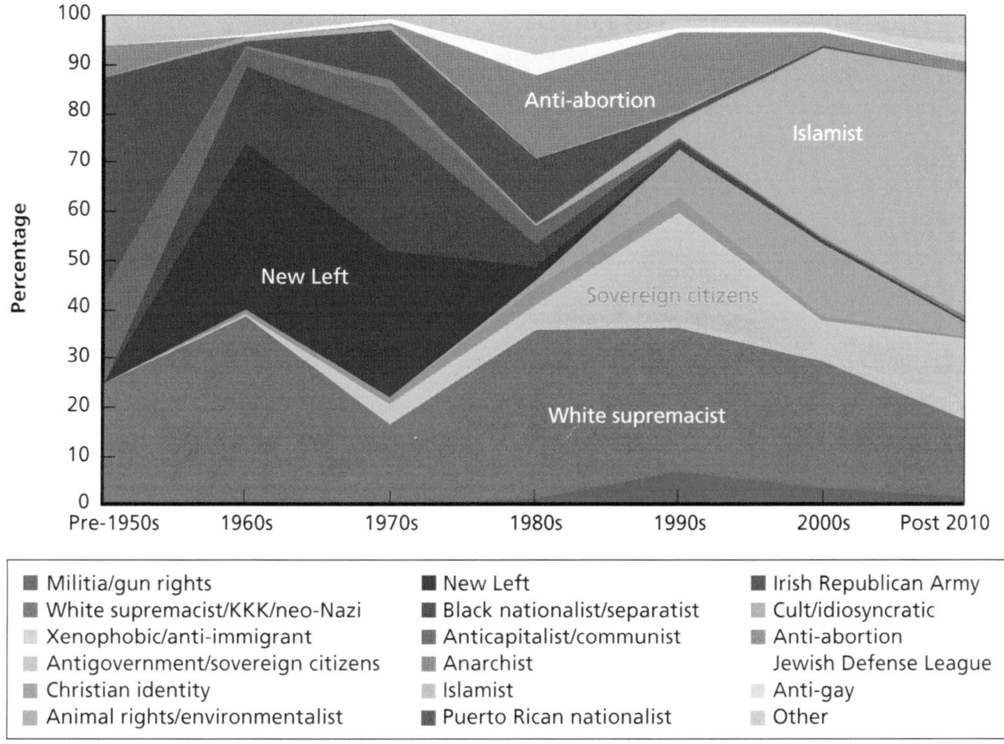

SOURCE: Data and ideology categories were drawn from the START PIRUS database. See START, undated(b).
NOTE: Data available at this writing end in 2016 and therefore do not reflect shifts occurring in 2017–2018. KKK = Ku Klux Klan.
RAND RR2647/2-1

high– and low–population density areas. Although certain communities or populations in the United States may be more susceptible to radicalization based on factors like poverty and lack of education, radicalization in the United States is more evenly distributed than it is in Europe, where identifiable pockets or neighborhoods are highly problematic and poorly integrated into the rest of society.[6]

From 2002 to 2016, PIRUS includes an average of just under 60 incidents of radicalization per year across all ideologies. Other analyses looking at individuals charged with terrorism-related offenses have focused only on jihadist terrorism—a subset of the

---

[6] START analysis of the characteristics of areas in which individuals who had planned and carried out violent incidents in the United States shows statistically significant differences between census tracts where their pre-incident activity had occurred and census tracts without such activity. Tracts with activity were lower in median income, had greater unemployment, and had a lower percentage of high school graduates. Although the differences were statistically significant, in most cases they were quite small. See START, 2013.

Figure 2
Locations of Individual Cases of Radicalization in the Continental United States Included in the PIRUS Database, 2002–2016

NOTE: Incidents are from START, undated(b), and are overlaid on U.S. Census population density by county.

RAND RR2647/2-2

incidents included in PIRUS. According to George Washington University (GWU) researchers' data as of May 2018, there have been 161 arrests related to individuals connected to ISIS in the United States since March 2014, yielding an average of approximately 40 arrests per year for just jihadist-inspired activity (GWU, 2018). New America, a think tank, conducted a survey of cases related to jihadist terrorism and found that 408 individuals have been killed or charged with jihadist terrorism–related offenses between 2001 and 2018 (Bergen et al., undated). Over approximately the same period as covered by the GWU data, New America's data suggest an average of approximately 45 cases per year. The New America data, which are presented by year, also illustrate the great variation in numbers of cases over time—some years with as few as five and one year (2015) with a high of 71 cases filed. As a result, depending on the relative contributions of other ideological sources of violence (e.g., applying data from PIRUS discussed earlier), these sources suggest an average number of incidents per year of between 50 and 100.

More-recent public statements by members of federal law enforcement and the intelligence community suggest higher numbers of arrests and ongoing investigations.[7] For example, 2017 testimony by FBI Director Christopher Wray cited a higher number than the academic literature of 176 arrests in the approximately 12 months preceding his remarks (Wray, 2017a; Wray, 2017b). In March 2018, Director Wray stated that there were 1,000 open jihadist-inspired homegrown extremist investigations as well as another 1,000 domestic investigations focused on threats from other ideologies (Wray, 2017a; Wray, 2017b; Williams, 2018).

Completed Attacks and Their Consequences

Although any terrorist incident within the United States raises concerns, the number of such incidents each year is relatively low, and the consequences of most such incidents are of commensurate scale. According to open-source data, there have been 329 such incidents between 2002 and 2016, with about half of these attacks occurring after 2011 (START, undated[a]). Over the full period, this corresponds to an average of approximately 22 attacks per year. From 2011 to 2016, this rate increased to about 33 attacks per year. Apart from clustering in large cities, there does not seem to be a clear geographic pattern for targets of attacks, with terrorist incidents having occurred in nearly every state.

According to the New America report on terrorism in America, 185 people have been killed in terrorist attacks on U.S. soil from late 2001 to 2018 (Bergen et al., undated).[8] This corresponds to approximately ten people per year killed as a result of terrorism in the years after 9/11, which is a much lower risk than many other sources of harm to people in the United States, from both violent and nonviolent sources.[9] The relatively low number of total deaths associated with attacks in the United States reflects the recent rarity of large-scale, mass-casualty events since 9/11. The United States has had incidents with more than ten fatalities since 9/11, including the San Bernardino and Pulse nightclub attacks. However, the United States has not had to endure

---

[7] Numbers of investigations are not a wholly independent measure of threat, since many factors can affect investigative activity that are separate from true threat levels (e.g., an increase in "terrorism tips" from the public will trigger more investigations, even if the tips are spurious). However, investigations divert law enforcement resources from responding to other types of violence and crime, and therefore their number is a measure of another facet of terrorism's effect on public safety and security.

[8] Note that this figure does not include the fatalities incurred by the attacks of 9/11, in which nearly 3,000 people were killed and hundreds more injured (Hoffman, 2017b).

[9] If 9/11 is included in the calculation of annual fatalities from terrorism in the United States—rather than limiting the scope to the period after those attacks, when CVE efforts in the United States were initiated and subsequently expanded—the average annual fatality rate increases to more than 170 people per year. Such a calculation clearly demonstrates the seriousness and scale of that event, but it also shows that simply averaging in such an incident with the subsequent 17 years, during which total fatalities were just more than 5 percent of the total number of individuals lost on 9/11, risks misrepresenting the intensity of ongoing terrorist risk to the country versus the risk of low-probability but high-consequence incidents.

multiple attacks killing hundreds of people, as has been the case for other nations in recent years, which has helped to limit the average annual burden of terrorism for the country. For example, the total number of U.S. fatalities over this period is less than the number of people killed in the March 2004 Madrid train bombings alone, in which 192 people died (Hoffman, 2017a).

Conclusions

Looking across available open-source data on threats to the United States and the assessment across the interviews carried out for the project—at both the national and local levels—we find an apparent consensus that the current terrorist threat to the United States is genuine but manageable, but that terrorism prevention could help to respond in more-efficient and practical ways. Sources of threat also are ideologically diverse, meaning that for terrorism prevention programs to maintain their value and relevance they cannot be ideologically specific, even as they must take into account and respond to the ideologies that are motivating individuals to pursue violence. The spread of the threat across the country also is a challenge, however, as individual cities or geographic areas will face small numbers of incidents of radicalization or attempted attacks, creating constraints to building and maintaining practical and acceptable terrorism prevention programming.

Current Terrorism Prevention Policies and Capabilities

If a nation chooses to pursue terrorism prevention policy, it requires clarity about what that policy is and what it is intended to do. It also needs to distinguish terrorism prevention from other approaches to responding to threats. Drawing on available government and other information, HSOAC defined the scope of terrorism prevention for the purposes of this analysis[10] as efforts that sought to

> reduce the incidence of violence inspired by ideology and extremist causes, and to expand the range of options for responding to that risk. It includes efforts—either alone or in collaboration—by such government entities as law enforcement, social services, and mental health agencies; non-governmental organizations; civil society; community groups; and the private sector.

---

[10] The study's definition was consistent with available definitions at the time, specifically NCTC, DHS, and FBI, 2017, and direction provided by DHS at the study's initiation. However, definitions of this policy area produced or used by multiple entities—not only DHS, but also individual law enforcement organizations, civil-society organizations, and others—could differ from our framing. It is our understanding that DHS is continuing to revise its definitions, goals, and objectives as the development of terrorism prevention policy and programming continues.

By building options beyond the traditional criminal justice tools of arrest, prosecution, and incarceration—and involving organizations and capabilities outside the organizational boundaries of government—terrorism prevention programs seek to enable action earlier, before individuals have taken illegal actions that could pose imminent danger and have lasting consequences both for themselves and others.

Applying this definition, we distinguished phases in the process by which an individual becomes radicalized to violence, and identified terrorism prevention activities to address each phase. We then used our understanding of these phases and the relevant populations for each to examine current terrorism prevention and past CVE efforts.

Phases of Radicalization to Violence

Given our current understanding of radicalization processes—and the near certainty of great diversity across individuals and among different causes and ideologies that might inspire violence—we chose to use a very basic model to anchor our work. We thus divided the people involved in radicalization processes into three relevant populations (see Figure 3):

- vulnerable population—i.e., all the people who might radicalize to violence
- individuals who are radical of thought but may or may not become violent
- individuals actually involved in attempted attacks (denoted by the red starburst in the figure).

The three populations are connected by two processes. The first process, moving from the early to the middle phase, involves radicalization to extremism, which may or may not mean a greater chance of the individual becoming violent. The second process, moving from the middle to the late phase, is mobilization to violence. Given the

Figure 3
Radicalization and Mobilization States, with Phases of Terrorism Prevention

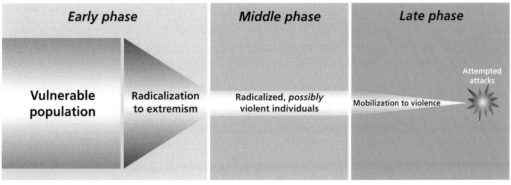

level of threat in the United States, each successive population is much smaller than the population preceding it, with only a small percentage of any vulnerable population radicalizing and only a percentage of that population escalating to violence (see the discussion in Snair, Nicholson, and Giammaria, 2017).

Types of Terrorism Prevention Activities

The different points in the overall radicalization and mobilization process are focused on different populations and thus involve distinct terrorism prevention activities. We grouped these activities into three phases, each with distinct goals:

- The *early* phase focuses broadly on vulnerable populations either to increase resistance to radicalization or to reduce factors like extremist messages in the environment. Such efforts might include online messaging and countermessaging, as well as other forms of community education and engagement.
- The *middle* phase includes activities focusing on individuals at risk of radicalization to violence. It aims to encourage referrals for intervention and effectively deliver intervention programming.
- The *late* phase addresses efforts aimed at individuals who have broken the law and are already involved in the criminal justice system. This phase aims to deliver services, often from within the federal prison system, that are effective in preventing future violence or criminal activity supporting violence.

Figure 4 shows the five types of federal terrorism prevention activities—organized according to the three phases just described—that we identified through our research and that served as the basis of our assessment of past CVE and current terrorism prevention efforts. For each type, we have listed examples of potential terrorism prevention activities.

Within these broad categories, there are myriad possibilities for the design and scope of individual terrorism prevention activities. It is possible to think about these activities along a spectrum of government involvement and level of specificity to terrorism risk. At one end are "indirect or community-centered initiatives" that may be entirely outside of government and may not even focus specifically on terrorism risk, such as a counseling program run by a community or religious organization aimed at youth issues, where extremism may be only one among many issues covered. At the other end are "direct or government-driven initiatives" in which government and law enforcement are involved and may even play a central role, such as a police-managed program to connect troubled youth to counseling in an effort to change their behavior and keep them out of the criminal justice system. Some efforts may involve extensive participation from community organizations and individuals, social services sectors inside and outside government, other government entities, and law enforcement. Depending on the circumstances in a local area, community-, social service–, or crimi-

Figure 4
Types of Terrorism Prevention Efforts and Example Activities

Early Phase	Middle Phase	Late Phase
✓ Countering extremist messaging online ✓ Community education, engagement, resilience, and risk-factor reduction	✓ Referral promotion ✓ Intervention	✓ Recidivism reduction

Examples
• Removal of online content advocating violence
• Online messaging to encourage communities to identify radicalized individuals for intervention
• Resources to assist families in helping relatives avoid radicalization to violence
• Coordination of information-sharing and collaboration across organizations
• Support to community youth and economic development programs
	Examples
	• Awareness-building about what sorts of behaviors raise concerns
	• Community education campaigns
	• Law enforcement training
	• Risk assessment of individuals referred
	• Programs to build local intervention capability
	• Support to existing nongovernmental intervention programs
		Examples
		• Programs within federal prisons, including
		  • psychological counseling
		  • religious counseling
		  • social support
		    • family counseling
		    • occupational counseling
		• Post-release programs

RAND RR2647/2-4

nal justice–managed terrorism prevention options might be entirely separate from one another, might collaborate while remaining independent, or might be part of one integrated, multidisciplinary program. These issues will be important as we discuss current terrorism prevention activities and consider options for strengthening the federal terrorism prevention capability.

Assessment of Current Terrorism Prevention Efforts

Overall, our analysis of published literature and interviews with individuals involved in past CVE and current terrorism prevention at the federal and local levels revealed major gaps in national terrorism prevention efforts. Shortfalls came not just from limited programmatic focus and resource investment since 2014, but also as a result of sustained opposition that tried to constrain or halt CVE efforts.

There have been some successes, including in community education and public-private partnerships, such as the Peer2Peer (P2P) program. Capacity to intervene with individuals at risk of carrying out ideological violence also has been built into some local programs. However, such successes are viewed as fragile, particularly because of concerns about whether the programs could be sustained.

Next, we highlight additional findings related to the five types of terrorism prevention activities shown in Figure 4.

Early Phase: Countering Extremist Messaging Online

Among our interviewees, there was consensus that there must be a federal role in countermessaging, as online propaganda is a central driver of terrorist threats in the country from all ideological sources. Beyond active efforts to coordinate with the technology industry regarding its activities, current government efforts to respond to extremist messaging in the United States were viewed by interviewees as quite limited, especially compared with what is happening internationally. However, multiple interviewees argued that increasing government investment in the activity could be problematic, given concerns about infringement on constitutionally protected rights and freedoms.

One exception to the limited government involvement in countermessaging is the FBI's 2015 "Don't Be a Puppet" campaign, which tries to explain terrorist recruitment pathways but has been broadly criticized for perpetuating stereotypes against Muslims and breeding suspicion over potentially innocuous activities, such as travel to countries like Germany, France, and Saudi Arabia (Camera, 2016). The reaction to that program was cited as an example of the difficulty of direct government involvement in messaging efforts. In contrast to the paucity of its U.S.-focused countermessaging activity, the U.S. government has engaged in internationally focused messaging efforts, led by the U.S. Department of State (DOS), for years. The Global Engagement Center leads DOS's counterpropaganda efforts, which were expanded with the fiscal year (FY) 2017 National Defense Authorization Act to include state-sponsored disinformation (DOS, undated).

Private-sector and NGO efforts aimed at online messaging are more prevalent, including efforts by such platform providers as Google and Facebook to remove extremist content and by NGOs dedicated to responding to and challenging that content when it appears. One example is the Institute for Strategic Dialogue, a London-based company that provides how-to guides for creating and promoting terrorism prevention campaigns and content, supports research on extremist trends, and gives grants to NGOs seeking to create online countermessaging campaigns.

Public-private partnerships are viewed as a less risky way for government involvement in countermessaging efforts. The P2P program, cosponsored by DHS, DOS, and the U.S. Department of Defense, funded university students to create campaigns to counter extremist narratives (DHS Office of Academic Engagement, 2016). P2P was cited repeatedly by interviewees as a success story in government cooperation with private organizations on countermessaging, although its domestic component was recently defunded. Many interviewees viewed the recent defunding as a significant missed opportunity to build on that success.

Although some online campaigns have demonstrated substantial reach, evidence is limited that those who engage with countermessaging content online have reduced risk of involvement in extremist violence. Furthermore, removal of content from main-stream sites can displace extremist content to smaller technology platforms that are harder to monitor and with less capability and capacity to respond.

Early Phase: Community Education, Engagement, Resilience, and Risk-Factor Reduction

Federal and other entities have devoted significant effort to community education and engagement. Our interviewees believed that these efforts have been valuable and in demand.

At the federal level, the DHS Civil Rights and Civil Liberties (CRCL) office was an early adopter of community engagement (DHS CRCL, 2011) and continues to hold regular roundtables with community leaders and federal, state, and local government officials regarding community civil rights concerns. DHS and DOJ worked together on the Building Communities of Trust program, which provides roundtables in urban areas to establish and develop trust among law enforcement, local multiagency intelligence fusion centers, and the communities they serve in order to address protection of communities from violence, suspicious activity reporting, and protection of civil rights and liberties (Information Sharing Environment, DHS, Nationwide SAR Initiative, and DOJ Community Oriented Policing Services, 2014).

Other examples of useful central programming efforts noted in interviews included community awareness briefings (CABs) delivered by staff from several agencies, interactions between federal staff—most commonly DHS and U.S. Attorney's Office staff—and local communities, and community resilience exercises (CREXs). The CABs and CREXs are multipurpose: They educate and provide awareness to help their audiences identify individuals at risk of radicalizing to violence and promote referral for intervention.

In most of the cities we visited, interviewees argued for expanded outreach and engagement efforts, especially those involving federal *field staff* in local areas.[11] However, staff reductions at DHS have constrained these efforts, leading to unmet demand for products like the CABs and CREXs delivered by DHS, NCTC, and other partners. One issue raised about both federal and nonfederal engagement and outreach efforts was the risk of stigmatizing communities—creating the impression that all members of a specific community are potential terrorists, when that is not the intention.

Although outreach and community education clearly fall within the scope of terrorism prevention, it is an open question as to how much broad-based resilience and risk factor–reduction efforts fall within DHS's terrorism prevention efforts rather than being treated as part of broader federal community policing, violence reduction, or public health initiatives. Such broad programs—which focus on education, employment, strengthening families, or societal functioning—were very popular with inter-

---

[11] This was also a recommendation of the DHS Homeland Security Advisory Council, 2016.

viewees, in part because they were not viewed as stigmatizing and could respond to multiple societal issues simultaneously.

Middle Phase: Referral Promotion

A specific component of education and training efforts in past CVE initiatives was focused on recognizing warning signs that an individual may be at risk of perpetrating ideologically motivated violence with the goal of increasing the likelihood that the individual could be referred for help before he or she acted. There have been significant efforts over many years by several parts of the federal government and by other organizations to encourage referral promotion through community and public education campaigns. The successful coordination and deconfliction of these many community awareness efforts was one of the achievements of the CVE Task Force that was regularly cited by interviewees. Our interviewees rated past and ongoing referral promotion efforts—done as part of community outreach and education—as helpful.

Given the role of local law enforcement in responding to incidents of violence, as well as in identifying individuals at risk of violent radicalization through day-to-day policing activities, training officers to recognize signs of radicalization toward violence has been a prominent concern. At the federal level, one of the earlier programs of this sort was the State and Local Anti-Terrorism Training program, administered by DOJ's Bureau of Justice Assistance (BJA). This program provided train-the-trainer, on-site, and online training to state and local law enforcement on terrorism-related issues (BJA, undated).

With respect to mechanisms for referrals, there are robust systems inside government for suspicious activity–type reporting. However, there are no uniform mechanisms for making referrals for intervention by the public, although ongoing DHS grants have funded local organizations in the early stages of building such capabilities.

In assessing the outcomes of existing efforts, although awareness building has been included in DHS's and others' education efforts, based on the data available to our study, it was difficult to assess the likelihood that an individual at risk of perpetrating ideological violence would be identified and referred for assistance in any specific geographic area.

Once individuals of potential concern are referred, there are some existing risk assessment tools aimed at ideologically motivated violence, although they have been developed with a focus on correctional settings (for more information, see Herzog-Evans, 2018). The United Kingdom uses the "Vulnerability Assessment Framework" derived from one of those tools for its Channel referral program, which is part of the country's CVE efforts (Lloyd and Dean, 2015, p. 49).

However, the effectiveness of the available tools is a concern. Because there are no unambiguous indicators of future violent behavior, risk assessment approaches cannot readily and reliably assess individual risk (RTI International, 2017a). However, just as local intervention efforts have referral paths in place, the programs operating in the cities we visited also had risk assessment processes that they viewed as workable for terrorism prevention efforts for small numbers of at-risk individuals. The assessment approaches were essentially all implemented with multidisciplinary teams, where different types of expertise were brought to bear to evaluate individual cases—but such approaches would have difficulty if the numbers of cases increased significantly.

Given the limitation of risk assessment, national performance for terrorism prevention would benefit most from efforts that increase true positive referrals (i.e., referrals of individuals who actually pose a risk of violence) more than simply increasing the total volume of referrals (i.e., true and false positives). The people who are most likely to know that an individual is at risk of carrying out violence are family, friends, and other individuals or professionals with close relationships with the person. As a result, the fundamental goal in referral promotion should be increasing referrals from them, rather than seeking more referrals or suspicious activity reporting from strangers. The willingness of family and friends to make such referrals requires the highest level of trust and depends on their belief that the programs to which they are reaching out have the capability to act and will try to help the individuals they refer.

Middle Phase: Intervention

Intervention is a central piece of what is required for terrorism prevention to achieve its goals: Without the capacity and capability to *help* an individual at risk of perpetrating ideological violence, success in community education, awareness, and referral promotion will have nothing to connect to, and the only option available to respond to someone will be arrest, prosecution, and incarceration.

Because of the inevitability that some individuals referred as possible threats will be false positives, intervention systems must be designed with the explicit goal of minimizing the negative effects of being referred on those individuals. Navigating that challenge is critical, as our interviewees characterized intervention as extremely vulnerable to concern about stigma and controversy if it is viewed as taking unjustified punitive action against individuals. Because of damaged trust in the federal government and concerns about government action focused on individuals whose actions may be worrisome but are not criminal, our interviewees generally believed that intervention must be managed predominantly at the local level.

Across our interviews at all levels, there was consensus that national capability to conduct interventions and respond to individuals at risk of perpetrating ideological violence is very limited. The only examples of federal activity in this area we identified were initiatives by the FBI and the U.S. Attorney's Office: the Shared Responsibility Committees (SRCs) and Disruption and Early Engagement Program (DEEP). The FBI described the SRCs, launched in 2016, as voluntary groups made up of law enforcement, family and community members, mental health professionals, and religious leaders to identify potential violent extremists for intervention (U.S. House of Representatives, 2016). Although some commended the Bureau for exploring new approaches to CVE, the SRCs were halted after significant criticism by civil rights organizations. Limited public information is available on the scope of the DEEP effort.

Federal entities also have encouraged and supported state and local models of intervention. For example, in September 2014, DOJ announced that it was launching a series of pilot programs (run in partnership with the White House, DHS, and NCTC) in three regional metropolitan areas—Boston, Los Angeles, and the Twin Cities of Minneapolis and St. Paul (DOJ, 2014; and DOJ, 2015). The program aimed to bring together community representatives, public safety officials, religious leaders, and U.S. government representatives to improve local engagement, counter violent extremism, and build a broad network of community partnerships to keep the country safe (DOJ, 2014). DHS also awarded three FY 2016 CVE grant efforts to build out intervention capacity in Oakland, Las Vegas, and Houston.

NGOs have sponsored several intervention efforts focused on specific communities or needs related to terrorism prevention. One such effort is by Life After Hate, which involves a crisis intervention initiative to help people move away from racism and violent extremism (Life After Hate, undated). Another is the World Organization for Resource Development and Education (WORDE)'s Build Resilience Against Violent Extremism (BRAVE) model (WORDE, 2016). Some government efforts at the local level also provide intervention capability for ideologically motivated violence risk. For example, the Los Angeles Police Department recently launched the Providing Alternatives to Hinder Extremism program, which aims to respond to individuals at risk of perpetrating violence and, working with the Mental Evaluation Unit, to intervene and provide counseling and other services to them. The program is nested within the broader approach taken in Los Angeles to address targeted violence.

Similarly, in other cities—including several visited for this study—the issue of intervention for ideologically motivated violence risk is addressed in the context of existing programs for other individuals or youth at risk of perpetrating violence for other reasons (e.g., mental health concerns, school violence). This is viewed as a pragmatic path, since the low incidence rate of terrorism in any local area makes building and maintaining dedicated programs impractical.

Although existing programs represent success stories for building intervention capability, these successes are viewed as fragile, driven in large part by the controversy surrounding past CVE and current terrorism prevention efforts and the limited available funding to support the efforts. The absence of more-robust intervention capacity also risks reinforcing perceptions by entities critical of past CVE efforts that referring individuals at risk of perpetrating ideological violence is more likely to lead to prosecution than counseling, representing an additional reason to strengthen capacity.

Late Phase: Recidivism Reduction

Analogous to intervention capacity, there also was consensus across our interviews that current recidivism-focused programming is not sufficient to meet the national need.

Previous strategies to respond to terrorism—including prosecution on such charges as material support—resulted in intermediate-length sentences for the individuals involved, and significant numbers of terrorism-convicted offenders are approaching release from prison.

Within correctional institutions, there is a menu of practices for approaching offender management to address risk. Programming within the prison context includes psychological counseling of various types; religious counseling and support (e.g., prison chaplaincy to counsel individuals whose extremist beliefs are linked to religious traditions); and various types of social support, including family counseling, occupational counseling, and other programming (UNODC, 2016, Chapters 5 and 8; Veldhuis, 2012). Specific interventions aimed at juveniles at risk of violent radicalization also have been developed (reviewed in Lefas and Nozawa, 2016). In the United States, all inmates in federal facilities (including those incarcerated for terrorism-related offenses) have access to a range of voluntary programs, including mental health counseling and therapy and educational programs. Interviewees also indicated that relevant agencies are assessing whether there is a need for programming specific to ideological violence.

In the probation and post-release environment, European countries in particular have developed CVE programming focused on reducing return to violence both by the formerly incarcerated and by individuals who have returned home after travel to fight in areas of conflict. The Radicalisation Awareness Network (RAN, 2017) and Global Counterterrorism Forum (undated) review several such programs that combine various types of counseling, involvement of family members or social network members in programming, and other supervision mechanisms. Efforts are being implemented in the United States for post-release supervision that have drawn on lessons from other countries' experiences. Although those efforts are providing capacity in specific regions of the country—and there are individuals under supervision who have been convicted of terrorism-related offenses arising from multiple ideological sources—overall national capacity for post-release supervision of terrorism-convicted offenders is still limited.

Across our interviewees, there was consensus regarding the need for more recidivism-focused programming. Although some programming is available, the view was that current efforts are not sufficient to meet the need, particularly with increasing numbers of individuals slated to be released from custody. Although the main population cited to support this need was post-9/11 jihadist-inspired offenders who will be reaching the end of their sentences within a few years, a similar argument would apply to individuals inspired by other ideologies.

Resources Allocated to Terrorism Prevention Efforts

One of the critiques of past U.S. CVE and current terrorism prevention efforts is that comparatively small amounts of money have been devoted to it compared with either counterterrorism as a whole or efforts to manage other safety and health risks. Although the exact amount spent on terrorism prevention per year governmentwide is difficult to determine with precision, it is clear that the total is small (in the tens of millions of dollars). Terrorism prevention spending is dwarfed by the amounts spent by the U.S. government on law enforcement and other direct counterterrorism efforts. Interviewees in our study characterized the level of expenditure as more consistent with an effort that is still experimenting and identifying policy approaches rather than implementing programing at scale.

We took three approaches to assessing different levels of U.S. investment in terrorism prevention and came to a similar conclusion in each case:

- Compared with other Western democracies, U.S. spending on terrorism prevention is at or below the bottom of funding ranges calculated based on different nations' levels of threat and well below the low end of ranges based on population.
- Because the traditional criminal justice approaches to counterterrorism of arrest, prosecution, and incarceration are expensive—and the costs of large numbers of even short preliminary investigations add up—even if terrorism prevention only makes it possible to reduce that activity by a modest percentage, the benefits will justify the programming costs.
- The conclusion is similar when approaching the problem looking at the costs of terrorist attacks. Because even small-scale terrorist attacks involve significant costs—in damage, loss of life, investigation, and recovery—if programs prevent only a few attacks, more-significant expenditures on terrorism prevention can be justified.

As a result, particularly in light of expenditures in the billions of dollars devoted to the rest of the nation's counterterrorism efforts, increases in terrorism prevention funding would not only put U.S. efforts in this policy area more in line with other nations, but also appear likely to pay off, even if they make only modest reductions in the burden of counterterrorism investigations on law enforcement or in numbers of attempted terrorist attacks.

Integration of Terrorism Prevention Efforts

The research found that there is work to be done to better integrate federal activities into a truly whole-of-government approach to terrorism prevention. During the latter phases of past CVE and current terrorism prevention efforts, interagency efforts were coordinated via the CVE Task Force. Multiple interviewees credited the Task Force structure with fixing several basic coordination problems that drove its creation (e.g., rationalizing across the multiple versions of the CABs that had been used by different federal agencies, reducing variation in messaging across state, local, and nongovernmental engagement efforts). However, interviewees also identified critical needs for the CVE Task Force, including bringing nonsecurity agencies more substantially into terrorism prevention efforts, addressing interagency incentive issues that create barriers to innovation and effectiveness, and better serving state and local stakeholders.

To strengthen terrorism prevention, stakeholders identified several core functional requirements necessary for a future structure to improve on past performance. First, there was consensus that terrorism prevention efforts needed top-level access and support from the leadership of participating agencies. Second, interviewees felt that, whatever coordination structure is chosen, driving experimentation and innovation should be a priority. Third, if bringing nonsecurity departments and agencies like the U.S. Department of Health and Human Services or the U.S. Department of Education more substantially and publicly into terrorism prevention initiatives is indeed a priority—which the frequency with which it was raised in our interviews suggests it should be—that goal will likely be a core driver in the design of the organization and the division of responsibilities. Fourth, interagency coordination requires bridging the boundary between classified and unclassified information, and having efficient mechanisms to develop readily sharable fully unclassified products. Finally, balancing operational- and enforcement-based activity versus efforts aimed at collaborative and community-centered approaches must be a priority for federal terrorism prevention efforts to be effective.

Federal Options to Strengthen Terrorism Prevention Capability

Design Challenges

We asked our interviewees about major issues or problems that future terrorism prevention programs would need to address to be effective in order to provide a basis for proposing future directions. We distilled that input into ten significant "design challenges," which we show in Table 1 and discuss in more detail later.

As indicated by the items in the list, federal terrorism prevention efforts need to be approached with practicality in mind. Despite attention to terrorism as a threat, for any specific city or area, ideologically motivated violence is a low-base-rate problem compared with issues like crime, drugs, and gangs. One consequence of this reality is the argument that, where possible, either terrorism prevention should be integrated into existing programs for responding to individuals at risk of committing violence more broadly or that terrorism prevention programs should be implemented so that they can serve the needs of broader populations (e.g., school violence) in addition to terrorism. As a result, while programming needs to be responsive to the specific ideologies that are inspiring violent action, programs that are highly specific to a particular ideology may be difficult to sustain.

Table 1
Challenges in Designing National Terrorism Prevention Efforts

Design Challenge	Description
1	Responding practically to the relatively low rate of radicalization, while also addressing the wide national dispersion of need
2	Navigating the tension between a need for efficiency, which could lead to an emphasis on specific communities, and the risk of stigmatizing communities and alienating key allies
3	Responding to variations in public trust, which can range from enthusiastic to strongly opposed
4	Managing the fact that the "damaged CVE brand" has frightened away important partners
5	Standardizing approaches in useful ways, while acknowledging that terrorism prevention activities must be highly specific to local circumstances
6	Coordinating independent multidisciplinary organizations with overlapping responsibilities while avoiding conflict between operational demands and more-collaborative terrorism prevention approaches
7	Mitigating risk aversion (including fears of failure and liability), which can limit experimentation and innovation
8	Developing terrorism prevention approaches that are not dependent on specific individuals and that can be sustained through staffing changes
9	Balancing the demand for data collection and measurement in terrorism prevention with the need to avoid reinforcing community perceptions of being surveilled and stigmatized
10	Using traditional federal policy levers of funding and influence in the controversial environment that surrounds terrorism prevention efforts

Identifying potential rare threats carries the inherent risk of false positives—i.e., people being viewed as potential threats who are not. This means that programs must be designed with the goal of minimizing both the costs to them and the chance of their being stigmatized as a result of their "participation" in a terrorism prevention program. Past controversy and intense suspicion of federal involvement in some communities have handicapped efforts from the outset. These concerns have scared away key potential partners and have made it difficult to build out terrorism prevention capabilities, and have even made some organizations reticent to accept federal grant dollars connected to the topic.

Strategy for Federal Terrorism Prevention Efforts

Given these challenges, what is the right strategy for the federal government and for DHS in particular? The study found that the most effective path for the federal government is to support state, local, nongovernmental, and private organizations' terrorism prevention efforts through funding and other approaches. Interviewees also emphasized that the federal government must approach terrorism prevention with patience. This is not a policy area where there is a short-term "silver bullet" policy solution, and it will take time to build consensus around acceptable and workable local approaches, but local success will translate to national success.

There was relatively strong consensus across all interviews that such efforts have to be locally designed, managed, and driven, and implemented in a way that is acceptable to the communities they are intended to protect. At the same time, having someone aware of the federal picture who is locally based can help to build relationships, strengthen trust, and act as an on-the-ground facilitator of local terrorism prevention efforts. This was viewed as an option that could deliver immediate results and help to build for the longer term. We found stark differences between cities with a dynamic, supported, and engaged federal field staff—where relationships were stronger and programs were more robust—and cities where such staff were absent.

There also was consensus among interviewees that a major part of what was required to broaden viable federal action for terrorism prevention was in how the topic is framed from the federal level, and whether local areas have the flexibility to reframe it in ways that are appropriate for their circumstances. We heard different variations of the message that "words matter" over and over again. Most interviewees illustrated this point by citing the view that, since the initiation of CVE at the federal level, although it has been said that all forms of extremism were covered, the main focus was on jihadist violence and, as a result, on Muslim communities. Most interviewees emphasized that terrorism prevention must include the threat of ideological violence from *all* sources—from ISIS to white supremacists to environmentally inspired violence—and must do so not only in statements, but also in programming and investment.

It is not clear that the federal government should take the further step argued by some interviewees at the local level and treat terrorism prevention as one component of general violence reduction and eliminate efforts specifically "branded" as focusing on terrorism. Increasing the involvement of nonsecurity agencies in terrorism prevention could yield some of the benefits of that proposal while maintaining terrorism prevention as a distinct program area. However, at the local level, it is clear that many organizations are already "mainstreaming terrorism prevention" into more-general initiatives that respond to individuals at risk of perpetrating violence, irrespective of how the federal government defines the problem, reflecting both what is practical for them and what is effective for their local communities.

Federal Policies and Options

We identified a robust menu of possible actions to support effective and practical federal policies and intervention options. These fall into four main categories of activity, and focus on enabling terrorism prevention initiatives from the bottom up and supporting the development of a national approach to this issue. There also are specific issues in individual elements of terrorism prevention (e.g., concerns about liability raised regarding intervention) where federal action could be beneficial, but these are more narrowly focused. We discuss each category of potential activities in turn, and summarize these options in Table 2.

Awareness and Training

A key role for the federal government is to provide credible information, including sharing of best practices and tools, to organizations seeking to implement terrorism prevention efforts. This was viewed as a good role for the federal government, from a desire for threat information by technology companies, to requests for more risk assessment information for corrections staff, to praise for CABs and CREXs from multiple directions. Sharing best practices and knowledge was similarly flagged as important, as was the value of bringing together researchers, implementers, and others to share information on terrorism prevention. In the course of the study, adaptation of existing tools (e.g., CREXs) to help empower local areas to explore the types of terrorism prevention that are appropriate for their circumstances appeared to be promising. All of these efforts—some building on past programs and initiatives—are options that could be included in future policy design.

We also heard arguments for more openness and transparency in terrorism prevention efforts so that critical audiences are reassured that these efforts are really doing what they say they are doing. In addition to helping to support trust in a controversial area, using unclassified and open source information that can be shared broadly is more practical for efforts that must bridge many organizational boundaries.

Federal Support of Local Initiatives

Another priority identified during the project is federal support of local initiatives, which could include support via such options as grant funding, public-private partnerships, or by helping communities identify programs and adopt locally designed terrorism prevention efforts. Given the difficulties associated with direct federal action in many elements of terrorism prevention, federal support of local initiatives appears to be necessary to advance efforts and build capacity. Public-private partnerships appear to be the best approach in terms of messaging and countermessaging. In many cases, continuing direct support to local programs through grants appears to be needed. A substantial investment in intervention capacity that is separate from law enforcement would be valuable, and would address previous criticism that CVE was not, in fact, providing alternatives to law enforcement action. There is also a need to broaden support from nonsecurity agencies, since doing so would enable both more-significant investment in areas that community interviewees prioritized and helping to address past concerns about CVE programs.

The federal government also can play a useful role in helping communities identify and implement the types of programs that work for them. This was often crystalized as "federal government as a convener"—i.e., getting people around a table to figure out what they needed and what was necessary to achieve their goals. Given the focus on federal field staff in the cities we visited, however, it was clear that this required much more than just getting the right people at the table. To be a *credible convener* and to navigate local complexities requires an individual with knowledge of terrorism prevention strategies and options as well as the ability to address the many design challenges noted earlier. This role also requires individuals who can build trust over time: Even if the federal government is giving away its help for free, the people providing that help have to be trusted enough that communities—including local government, service providers, and citizens—want what they are providing.

Federal Program Development

Most options identified in this analysis are not about new federal programs. Some involve continuing or revitalizing current federal terrorism prevention efforts. Funding and programmatic support would be needed to put federal field staff in place and to support them in playing their facilitating roles. Providing some types of support to local initiatives would require the continuation of a grant program that can fund initiatives where local resources are not sufficient.

The main programmatic exception to this is in the area of recidivism reduction, where the central role of the federal prison system in managing terrorism-related offenders means that any expansion of capabilities would require action at the federal level. Another issue where the federal government is best positioned to respond is human capital: the development of people—both inside government and in the research and service-provider sectors—who are both engaged in and knowledgeable about terrorism prevention. Such issues are more likely to be addressed in the course of other federal activities (e.g., investments in public-private partnerships, research, or program implementation) rather than through a stand-alone effort, but building and maintaining the bench of expert practitioners in this area was viewed as important by our interviewees from the national to the local levels.

Situational Awareness and Research and Evaluation

The federal government also can play a key role in data-gathering and analysis. Managing terrorism prevention efforts requires sustained data collection to provide situational awareness and guide analysis because, as one of our interviewees put it, "Unlike the Bureau of Justice Statistics in the Department of Justice, there is no Bureau of Homeland Security Statistics" (interview with a federal-level representative, 2018). Key situational awareness requirements include tracking public views and concerns and assessing the capacity of national intervention and other systems. Beyond those efforts, other research and evaluation requirements appear across the range of terrorism prevention elements: Our interviewees and literature sources called out the need for better measurement and evaluation (as well as better integration of evaluation into programs as they are implemented), and research on the sustainability of terrorism prevention efforts. They also noted the enduring challenge of individual risk assessment for ideologically motivated violence. Investments in any or all of these options could benefit the design, implementation, and evaluation of future programs. Both interviewees and authors of published literature argued that a more robust and interdisciplinary research community is needed for terrorism prevention (and was needed through past CVE efforts as well). Although existing efforts are viewed as useful (e.g., NCTC's annual CVE conference), they are not enough (multiple interviews at the national and local levels, 2018; also RTI International, 2017b; Rosand, 2017; and Levitt, 2017). Strengthening investment in evaluation also would respond to criticism of the effectiveness of both past CVE and current terrorism prevention efforts.

Conclusion

The timing of this study, with the changeover in administrations, presents an opportunity to look at what had been done before and explore paths forward. When we integrated available information on both national and local CVE and terrorism prevention initiatives, the picture that emerged was one of an effort still at an early stage. If greater consensus can be achieved regarding appropriate ways to build non–criminal justice approaches to dealing with terrorism risk, that process could help move toward better national policies.

To that end, the federal policy options laid out here have in part responded to issues raised during early efforts to develop then-CVE programs, drawing on examples from localities that have built approaches that seek to safeguard the rights and meet the needs of individuals potentially at risk of committing ideological violence, while still protecting society from potential terrorist attack. In doing so, the goal is to provide a set of options for *effective* policies and intervention options, but also *practical* ones, which respond appropriately to terrorism risk but do so in a way that simultaneously minimizes the manifold costs to the individuals affected and the society that terrorism prevention efforts aim to protect.

Table 2
Summary of Policy Options by Terrorism Prevention Activity and Category

Category	Countering Extremist Messaging Online	Community Education, Engagement, Resilience, and Risk Factor Reduction	Referral Promotion	Intervention	Recidivism Reduction
Awareness and Training	• Provide threat information to technology firms to support their countermessaging efforts • Increase technical staff in government terrorism prevention efforts to support outreach to industry. • Increase transparency of efforts and broadly share information for terrorism prevention purposes.	• Continue and expand outreach and local coordination efforts through CABs and CREXs.	• Continue and expand outreach and local coordination efforts through CABs and CREXs.	• Continue federal efforts to assemble and disseminate best practices and standards for intervention programs.	• Develop a customized CAB for corrections staff at the federal, state, and local levels. • When appropriate, develop training to disseminate best practices and new evidence-based practices in the corrections sector.

Table 2—Continued

Category	Countering Extremist Messaging Online	Community Education, Engagement, Resilience, and Risk Factor Reduction	Referral Promotion	Intervention	Recidivism Reduction
Federal Support of Local Initiatives	• Use grant funding to support counternarrative activities outside government.	• Make "on-call experts" with knowledge, program design, and evaluation expertise available to support local terrorism prevention initiatives. • Use grant funding to support local and NGO early-phase terrorism prevention activities. • Expand use of table-top exercises to assist localities in developing acceptable and practical local approaches to terrorism prevention.	• Continue to support efforts to develop national-level hotlines for referral of at-risk individuals. • Use grant funding to support local and NGO referral promotion efforts, but recognize that substantial trust-building may be required.	• Use grant funding to support local and NGO intervention models and networks. • Make "on-call experts" with knowledge, program design, and evaluation expertise available to support local terrorism prevention initiatives. • Prioritize supporting intervention capacity separate from law enforcement organizations, particularly in areas where trust is weakened. • Explore alternative funding mechanisms for local initiatives.	• Use grant funding to support state, local, and NGO implementation of recidivism-reduction programs.

Table 2—Continued

Category	Countering Extremist Messaging Online	Community Education, Engagement, Resilience, and Risk Factor Reduction	Referral Promotion	Intervention	Recidivism Reduction
Federal Program Development	• N/A	• Reconstitute and expand federal field staff to act as primary focal points for terrorism prevention at the local level.	• N/A	• Reconstitute and expand federal field staff to act as primary focal points for terrorism prevention at the local level.	• Coordinate with (and assist, as appropriate) federal corrections agencies developing recidivism reduction programming. • Support the development of programs for terrorism prevention intervention efforts to maintain effectiveness across the country.
Situational Awareness	• Sustain efforts to characterize the extent of extremist content online on an ongoing basis. • Publicly release results of the content census to enable public action.	• N/A	• Support periodic, publicly released national surveys to assess public willingness to refer individuals because of concern regarding early mobilization activities.	• Gather data on existing capabilities relevant to terrorism prevention intervention nationally to help facilitate network development and identify shortfalls.	• Develop and maintain a centralized database of individuals incarcerated for ideological violence-related offenses to support program development and implementation.

Table 2—Continued

Category	Countering Extremist Messaging Online	Community Education, Engagement, Resilience, and Risk Factor Reduction	Referral Promotion	Intervention	Recidivism Reduction
Regulatory and Legal Issues	• N/A	• N/A	• Address perceived legal and regulatory barriers to interagency collaboration in terrorism prevention referral and intervention.	• Address perceived legal and liability barriers to nongovernmental intervention activities.	• N/A
Research and Evaluation	• Continue to invest in evaluation of counter-narrative efforts.	• Support periodic, publicly released national surveys to assess knowledge and awareness about radicalization and mobilization to violence.	• Continue research focused on improving risk-assessment methods, but manage expectations for their possible accuracy.	• Continue to invest in evaluation of intervention programs. • Prioritize research and evaluation efforts to better understand factors affecting the sustainability of terrorism prevention intervention programs.	• Continue to invest in evaluation of recidivism-reduction programs. • Continue research focused on improving risk-assessment methods, but manage expectations for their possible accuracy. • Prioritize focused research and evaluation efforts to better understand the effect of incarceration on radicalization and violence risk.

Table 2—Continued

Category	Countering Extremist Messaging Online	Community Education, Engagement, Resilience, and Risk Factor Reduction	Referral Promotion	Intervention	Recidivism Reduction
Auxiliary Federal Activities	• N/A	• Recognize and pro-actively manage effects that other DHS and federal programs can have on community trust to support terror-ism prevention initiatives. • Increase interagency investment separate from terrorism pre-vention initiatives to address community concerns and reduce risk factors related to radicalization to violence.	• N/A	• N/A	• N/A

NOTE: N/A = not applicable.

References

American Civil Liberties Union, "ACLU Briefing Paper: What Is Wrong with the Government's 'Countering Violent Extremism' Programs," undated. As of October 5, 2018: https://www.aclu.org/other/aclu-v-dhs-briefing-paper

Bergen, Peter, Albert Ford, Alyssa Sims, and David Sterman, *Terrorism in America After 9/11*, Washington, D.C.: New America, undated. As of October 5, 2018: https://www.newamerica.org/in-depth/terrorism-in-america/

BJA—*See* Bureau of Justice Assistance.

Bureau of Justice Assistance, *State and Local Anti-Terrorism Training (SLATT) Program*, Washington, D.C.: U.S. Department of Justice, undated. As of October 5, 2018: https://www.bja.gov/ProgramDetails.aspx?Program_ID=120

Camera, Lauren, "FBI's Anti-Extremism Website Should Be Scrapped, Groups Say," *U.S. News and World Report*, April 6, 2016. As of October 5, 2018: https://www.usnews.com/news/articles/2016-04-06/ fbi-dont-be-a-puppet-website-criticized-by-advocacy-groups

DHS—*See* U.S. Department of Homeland Security.

DHS CRCL—*See* U.S. Department of Homeland Security, Civil Rights and Civil Liberties Office.

DOJ—*See* U.S. Department of Justice.

DOS—*See* U.S. Department of State.

George Washington University, Program on Extremism, "GW Extremism Tracker: The Islamic State in America," infographic, May 7, 2018. As of October 5, 2018: https://extremism.gwu.edu/sites/g/files/zaxdzs2191/f/May%202018%20Tracker.pdf

Global Counterterrorism Forum, *Rome Memorandum on Good Practices for Rehabilitation and Reintegration of Violent Extremist Offenders*, undated.

GWU—*See* George Washington University.

Herzog-Evans, Martine, "A Comparison of Two Structured Professional Judgment Tools for Violent Extremism and Their Relevance in the French Context," *European Journal of Probation*, Vol. 10, No. 1, 2018.

Hoffman, Bruce, "The Evolving Terrorist Threat and Counterterrorism Options of the Trump Administration," *The Georgetown Security Studies Review*, February 24, 2017a, pp. 6–14. As of October 5, 2018: http://georgetownsecuritystudiesreview.org/wp-content/uploads/2017/02/Hoffman-The-Evolving-Terrorist-Threat-and-Counterterrorism-Options-for-the-Trump-Administration.pdf

———, "A Growing Terrorist Threat on Another 9/11: Al Qaeda Has Regrouped Even as the Battered Islamic State Remains Lethal," *Wall Street Journal*, September 8, 2017b. As of October 5, 2018:
https://www.wsj.com/articles/a-growing-terrorist-threat-on-another-9-11-1504888986

Information Sharing Environment, Department of Homeland Security, Nationwide Suspicious Activity Reporting Initiative, U.S. Department of Justice Community Oriented Policing Services, *Building Communities of Trust Fact Sheet*, January 2014. As of October 5, 2018:
https://www.dhs.gov/sites/default/files/publications/Building%20Communities%20of%20Trust.pdf

Lefas, Melissa, and Junko Nozawa, *Rehabilitating Juvenile Violent Extremist Offenders in Detention: Advancing a Juvenile Justice Approach*, The Hague, Netherlands: International Centre for Counter-Terrorism, Global Center on Cooperative Security, December 2016.

Levitt, Matthew, ed., *Defeating Ideologically Inspired Violent Extremism: A Strategy to Build Strong Communities and Protect the U.S. Homeland*, Washington, D.C.: Washington Institute for Near East Policy, No. 37, March 2017.

Life After Hate, homepage, undated. As of October 29, 2018:
https://www.lifeafterhate.org

Lloyd, Monica, and Christopher Dean, "The Development of Structured Guidelines for Assessing Risk in Extremist Offenders," *Journal of Threat Assessment and Management*, Vol. 2, No. 1, 2015.

National Consortium for the Study of Terrorism and Responses to Terrorism, "Global Terrorism Database," database, undated(a). As of October 5, 2018:
https://www.start.umd.edu/gtd/

———, "Profiles of Individual Radicalization in the United States (PIRUS)," dataset, undated(b). As of October 5, 2018:
http://www.start.umd.edu/data-tools/profiles-individual-radicalization-united-states-pirus

———, *From Extremist to Terrorist: Identifying the Characteristics of Communities Where Perpetrators Live and Pre-Incident Activity Occurs Prior to Attacks: Report to the Resilient Systems Division, Science and Technology Directorate, U.S. Department of Homeland Security*, College Park, Md., April 2013.

———, *Profiles of Individual Radicalization in the United States (PIRUS) Codebook: Public Release Version*, College Park, Md., January 2018. As of October 5, 2018:
http://www.start.umd.edu/sites/default/files/files/research/PIRUSCodebook.pdf

National Counter Terrorism Center, U.S. Department of Homeland Security, and Federal Bureau of Investigation, "First Responders Toolbox: Terrorism Prevention—A Form of Violence Reduction," October 30, 2017. As of October 5, 2018:
https://www.dni.gov/files/NCTC/documents/jcat/firstresponderstoolbox/
First-Responders-Toolbox---Terrorism-PreventionA-Form-of-Violence-Reduction.pdf

NCTC—*See* National Counter Terrorism Center.

Radicalisation Awareness Network, *Preventing Radicalisation to Terrorism and Violent Extremism: Approaches and Practices*, Brussels, Belgium, 2017. As of October 5, 2018:
https://ec.europa.eu/home-affairs/sites/homeaffairs/files/what-we-do/
networks/radicalisation_awareness_network/ran-best-practices/docs/
ran_collection-approaches_and_practices_en.pdf

RAN—*See* Radicalisation Awareness Network.

Rosand, Eric, "Fixing CVE in the United States Requires More than Just a Name Change," Brookings Institution blog, February 16, 2017. As of October 5, 2018:
https://www.brookings.edu/blog/order-from-chaos/2017/02/16/
fixing-cve-in-the-united-states-requires-more-than-just-a-name-change/

RTI International, *Countering Violent Extremism: The Use of Assessment Tools for Measuring Violence Risk, Literature Review*, Research Triangle Park, N.C., March 2017a. As of October 5, 2018:
https://www.dhs.gov/sites/default/files/publications/OPSR_TP_CVE-Use-Assessment-Tools-Measuring-Violence-Risk_Literature-Review_March2017-508.pdf

———, *Countering Violent Extremism (CVE)—Developing a Research Roadmap: Final Report*, Research Triangle Park, N.C., October 2017b. As of October 5, 2018:
https://www.dhs.gov/sites/default/files/publications/
861_OPSR_TP_CVE-Developing-Research-Roadmap_Oct2017.pdf

Snair, Justin, Anna Nicholson, and Clair Giammaria, *Countering Violent Extremism Through Public Health Practice: Proceedings of a Workshop*, Washington, D.C.: National Academies Press, 2017.

START—*See* National Consortium for the Study of Terrorism and Responses to Terrorism.

United Nations Office of Drugs and Crime, *Handbook on the Management of Violent Extremist Prisoners and the Prevention of Radicalization to Violence in Prisons*, New York: United Nations, 2016.

UNODC—*See* United Nations Office of Drugs and Crime.

U.S. Department of Homeland Security, Civil Rights and Civil Liberties Office, "Newsletter," Vol. 2, No. 1, September 2011. As of October 5, 2018:
http://www.aila.org/infonet/dhs-crcl-september-2011-newsletter

U.S. Department of Homeland Security, Homeland Security Advisory Council, "Interim Report and Recommendations," Washington, D.C., Countering Violent Extremism (CVE) Subcommittee, June 2016.

U.S. Department of Homeland Security, Office of Academic Engagement, "How DHS Partnerships Help Counter Violent Extremism," DHS Study in the States blog, July 20, 2016. As of October 5, 2018:
https://studyinthestates.dhs.gov/2016/07/how-dhs-partnerships-help-counter-violent-extremism

U.S. Department of Justice, "Attorney General Holder Announces Pilot Program to Counter Violent Extremists," press release, September 15, 2014. As of October 5, 2018:
https://www.justice.gov/opa/pr/
attorney-general-holder-announces-pilot-program-counter-violent-extremists

———, "Pilot Programs Are Key to Our Countering Violent Extremism Efforts," press release, February 18, 2015. As of October 5, 2018:
https://www.justice.gov/archives/opa/blog/
pilot-programs-are-key-our-countering-violent-extremism-efforts

U.S. Department of State, "Global Engagement Center," webpage, undated. As of October 5, 2018:
https://www.state.gov/r/gec

U.S. House of Representatives, Committee on Homeland Security, "Correspondence: FBI Shared Responsibility Committees Must Pass Privacy Test," 114th Congress, 2nd Session, April 29, 2016. As of October 5, 2018:
https://democrats-homeland.house.gov/sites/democrats.homeland.house.gov/files/sitedocuments/
pclobletter.pdf

Veldhuis, Tinka, *Designing Rehabilitation and Reintegration Programmes for Violent Extremist Offenders: A Realist Approach*, The Hague, Netherlands: International Centre for Counter-Terrorism, March 2012. As of October 5, 2018:
https://www.icct.nl/download/file/
ICCT-Veldhuis-Designing-Rehabilitation-Reintegration-Programmes-March-2012.pdf

Williams, Pete, "FBI Chief on Biggest Threats: China Spies, Terror, Rise in Violent Crime," *NBC News*, March 21, 2018. As of October 5, 2018:
https://www.nbcnews.com/politics/justice-department/
fbi-chief-biggest-threats-china-spies-terror-rise-violent-crime-n858786

World Organization for Resource Development and Education, *Building Resilience Against Violent Extremism*, 2016.

Wray, Christopher, "Responses to Congressional Questions: Homeland Security Threats," video testimony before the Senate Homeland Security and Governmental Affairs Committee, video, September 27, 2017a. As of October 5, 2018:
https://www.c-span.org/video/?434411-1/
senior-officials-testify-homeland-security-threats&start=1902

Wray, Christopher A., "Threats to the Homeland: Statement of Christopher A. Wray, Director, Federal Bureau of Investigation," testimony before the Senate Homeland Security and Government Affairs Committee, September 27, 2017b.